!NSPiRE

KATIE LEDECKY

BY JOE TISCHLER

AMICUS LEARNING

Inspire is published by
Amicus Learning, an imprint of Amicus
P.O. Box 227
Mankato, MN 56002
www.amicuspublishing.us

Editor: Aidan Whitcomb and Megan Siewert
Series Designer: Kathleen Petelinsek
Book Designer: Kim Pfeffer

Library of Congress Cataloging-in-Publication Data
Names: Tischler, Joe, author.
Title: Katie Ledecky / by Joe Tischler.
Description: Mankato, MN : Amicus Learning, [2025] | Series: Inspire | Includes bibliographical references and index. | Audience: Ages 5-9 | Audience: Grades 2-3 | Summary: "Learn about Olympics superstar Katie Ledecky and her accomplishments in swimming in this biography packed with action photos and fact-filled text suitable for young readers. Includes table of contents, glossary, further resources, and index"-- Provided by publisher.
Identifiers: LCCN 2023046009 (print) | LCCN 2023046010 (ebook) | ISBN 9781645499084 (library binding) | ISBN 9781645499169 (paperback) | ISBN 9781645499244 (ebook)
Subjects: LCSH: Ledecky, Katie, 1997---Juvenile literature. | Women swimmers--United States--Biography--Juvenile literature. | Swimmers--United States--Biography--Juvenile literature. | Women Olympic athletes--United States--Biography--Juvenile literature. | Olympic athletes--United States--Biography--Juvenile literature.
Classification: LCC GV838.L43 T57 2025 (print) | LCC GV838.L43 (ebook) | DDC 797.2/1092 [B]--dc23/eng/20231023
LC record available at https://lccn.loc.gov/2023046009
LC ebook record available at https://lccn.loc.gov/2023046010

Photo Credits: AP Newsroom/KYDPL KYODO, Cover, Mo Khursheed, 6; Dreamstime/Pavel Byrkin, 14; Getty/Al Bello, 8, Alexander Hassenstein, 21, Harry How, 11, Jean Catuffe, 15, John W. McDonough, 12, Paul Morigi, 19, Richard Heathcote, 20, Tom Pennington, 16-17, YUICHI YAMAZAKI, 5; Shutterstock/vicgmyr, 13; Wikimedia Commons/PoolSafely, 18

Table of Contents

4 Number One

7 Swimming Family

9 Young Star

10 Gold and Silver

13 Off to College

14 Back to the Games

16 Record Holder

18 Role Model

21 Future Goals

22 Super Stats

23 Glossary

24 Read More

24 On the Web

24 Index

Katie Ledecky has reset the standards of women's swimming.

Number One

Take your marks ... BANG! Katie Ledecky dives into the pool. She swims fast. She passes the other swimmers. First place!

Ledecky is one of the world's greatest swimmers. She has won nine **Olympic** gold **medals**!

LEDECKY

Ledecky has been swimming since a young age. Here, she is only 14 years old, celebrating a win.

Swimming Family

Ledecky began swimming at age six. She swam for a summer team. Her older brother was on the team. Katie's mother was also a swimmer. She swam in college.

Ledecky was the youngest Team USA athlete to participate in the 2012 Olympics.

Young Star

In high school, Ledecky broke many national swim records. At age 15, she swam in the 2012 Olympics. Those were held in London. There, she won her first Olympic gold medal! It was in the 800-meter **freestyle**. She won by more than four seconds.

HIGH SCHOOL GREATNESS

Ledecky holds nearly all swim records at her high school.

Gold and Silver

Ledecky did even better at the 2016 Rio Olympics. She won four gold medals. She set two world records! Those were in the 400- and 800-meter freestyle. She also won a silver medal on a relay team.

LEADING WOMAN

Ledecky's four gold medals tied the record for the most gold medals won by a U.S. female athlete in a single Olympics.

Ledecky won five medals at the 2016 Rio Olympics.

In her first year of college, Ledecky helped lead Stanford to their first national swimming title in nearly 20 years.

Off to College

After the Olympics, Ledecky went to college. She went to Stanford University. She broke 12 NCAA records her first year. She swam on the team there for two years. Stanford won national team **titles** both seasons.

COLLEGE GRAD
Ledecky graduated in 2021. She earned a **degree** in psychology.

Back to the Games

Ledecky won four more medals at the 2020 Tokyo Olympics. Two were gold! They were in the 800- and 1500-meter freestyle. She also got two silver medals. She has won 14 Olympic medals.

MEDAL WINNER

As of 2024, Ledecky has the most Olympic gold medals by a female swimmer.

Ledecky takes off for the 1500-m freestyle race at the 2020 Tokyo Olympics.

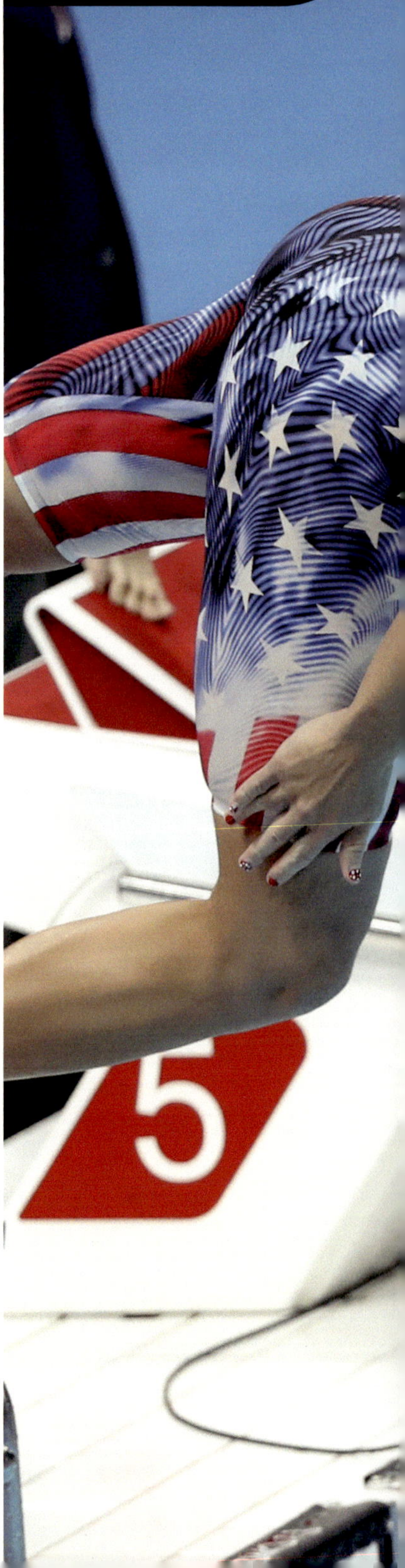

CHN
LEDECKY
6
7
OMEGA
OMEGA

Record Holder

As of 2023, Ledecky holds two world records. Those are in the 800- and 1500-meter freestyle. She has won 17 individual gold medals at the World Aquatics Championships. That's also a record!

Role Model

Ledecky is a role model outside of the water, too. She visits schools. She talks about the importance of learning. She tells kids to set goals both inside and outside the classroom.

Ledecky has worked with kids to teach them pool safety.

Ledecky attends events and benefits to set an example for her fans.

Ledecky trains nine times a week. Her training lasts two to three hours every day.

Future Goals

Ledecky still loves training in the pool. She can't wait for the next challenge. She wants to work harder than everybody else. She hopes to add more medals and records at the 2028 LA Olympics.

Ledecky's teammates cheer as they win the silver medal in the 4 x 200 freestyle relay at the 2020 Tokyo Olympics.

SUPER STATS

KATIE LEDECKY

Born: March 17, 1997

Hometown: Bethesda, Maryland

Birthplace: Washington, D.C.

College: Stanford University

AWARDS

14 Olympic medals:
9 gold, 4 silver, 1 bronze

26 World Aquatics Championship medals:
21 gold, 5 silver

World-record holder:
800-, 1500-meter freestyle

NCAA team champion:
2 times

NCAA individual champion:
8 times

Most individual world swimming titles:
16

GLOSSARY

degree An academic honor awarded to a student by a university after the completion of a course of study.

freestyle The fastest swimming stroke used in competitions, also known as "front crawl."

medal An award given to top performers in an athletic competition.

Olympics An international, multi-sport event that takes place every four years.

title A championship or award for winning a major sports competition.

READ MORE

Bolte, Mari. **Aquatics.** Mankato, Minn.: Creative Education and Creative Paperbacks, 2024.

Fishman, Jon M. **Katie Ledecky.** Minneapolis: Lerner Publications, 2021.

Mattern, Joanne. **12 Reasons to Love Swimming.** Mankato, Minn.: 12-Story Library, 2021.

ON THE WEB

USA Swimming
https://www.usaswimming.org/meet-the-team/national-team-roster

World Aquatics
https://www.worldaquatics.com/athletes/1002483/katie-ledecky/profile

INDEX

college, 7, 12, 13
family, 7
freestyle, 9, 10, 14, 16, 17, 21
medals, 4, 10, 11, 14, 17, 21
  gold, 4, 9, 10, 14
  silver, 10, 14, 21
Olympics
  London, 9
  Paris, 21
  Rio, 10, 11
  Tokyo, 14, 21
World Aquatic Championship, 17
world record 10, 17

About the Author

Joe Tischler is an editor, sports journalist, and avid sports fan living in Minnesota. He has written about high school, collegiate, and professional games for newspapers. His favorite teams are the Twins, Vikings, Timberwolves, and Golden Gophers.